WRITE ABOUT LIFE SCIENCE

The Test Connection

Grades 6–8

By
Mary Rose Hassinger

Published by Frank Schaffer Publications
an imprint of

 **Children's Publishing**

Editor: Mary Rose Hassinger

 **Children's Publishing**

Published by Frank Schaffer Publications
An imprint of McGraw-Hill Children's Publishing
Copyright © 2004 McGraw-Hill Children's Publishing

Send all inquiries to:
McGraw-Hill Children's Publishing
3195 Wilson Drive NW
Grand Rapids, Michigan 49544

Write About Life Science—grades 6–8
ISBN: 0-7424-1917-7

1 2 3 4 5 6 7 8 9 MAZ 09 08 07 06 05 04 03
The *McGraw-Hill* Companies

Table of Contents

Teacher Introduction

A teacher once asked her class, "If you discovered a cure for an incurable disease but could not communicate it to anyone else, would your discovery have value?" The class considered her question and then responded, "No." Being able to communicate through writing is an inherent trait of humans. It allows us to transcend many boundaries to get our point across or to make an important discovery known. Writing across the curriculum has become a target area as we seek to improve literacy skills in all content areas.

Scientists have relied on communicating their ideas and discoveries through writing since the study of science began. By keeping detailed journals of their experiments and data, scientists were able to pass on their knowledge to others. Sir Isaac Newton once said, "If I have seen further than others, it is because I have stood on the shoulders of giants." He knew the importance of reading and evaluating others' work to propel his own. Students need to be aware that science is a process and that the knowledge they read about in textbooks evolved over time through the work and efforts of many who relied on writing skills to ensure that their discoveries were recorded. *Write About Life Science* provides teachers with a valuable resource to help facilitate writing in the science arena.

Each reading selection is linked to the National Standards as outlined on pages 5 and 6. Each reading focuses on scientific inquiry and content standards. All readings are followed by a variety of writing activities, including synthesizing definitions, applying and recalling what was read, and summarizing main ideas. By completing the reading selections the vocabulary sheets together, students will be well prepared for the rest of the writing experiences. Writing strategies such as concept webs, cause and effect, compare and contrast, Venn diagrams, and interpretation diagrams are used to help improve students' writing skills. An experiment is often detailed in the readings to allow students to analyze and interpret data, draw conclusions, make inferences, and evaluate the steps of the scientific method used in inquiry-based science. Data provided in the experiments is derived from actual investigations or history. If desired, teachers can facilitate the lab or the project and have students collect their own data to analyze. Also included is a cumulative sample test. It has a variety of questions directly related to the reading selections in *Writing About Life Science*.

Readings and writing activities provided can be linked to current study, can be used as supplemental materials, can be integrated with other core subjects, or can stand alone. *Writing About Life Science* is a tool teachers can use to help prepare students for the types of experiences found in standardized tests. When students are provided scientific material in a format they can relate to, they gain a clearer understanding that science is more than a textbook filled with facts.

Standards Grid

National Standards: Scientific Inquiry: Grades 5–8	Pages
Identify questions directed toward objects or phenomenon that can be described, explained, or predicted through a scientific investigation.	All pages
Design, conduct, and evaluate an investigation; then interpret the data collected, use the evidence to generate explanations, propose alternative explanations, and critique explanations and procedures.	All pages
Use appropriate tools and techniques to gather, analyze, and interpret data collected in a scientific investigation.	All pages
Develop descriptions, explanations, predictions, and models providing causes for effects and establishing relationships based on evidence and logical argument.	All pages
Think critically and logically to make relationships between evidence and explanations by reviewing data from a simple experiment, summarizing the data, and forming a logical cause-and-effect relationship in the experiment.	All pages
National Standards: Life Science: Grades 5–8	
Living systems at all levels of organization (cells, organs, tissues) demonstrate the complementary nature of structure and function.	25, 26, 27, 28, 30, 49, 50
All organisms are made up of cells. Cells carry on many functions needed to sustain life.	25, 26, 27, 28, 29, 30, 31, 49, 50
Specialized cells perform specialized functions such as that of the muscles and heart.	30, 49, 50, 51, 52 53, 54, 55, 56
The human organism has numerous systems for bodily functions, and they all interact with one another.	49, 50, 51
Diseases are either the intrinsic failure of a system or the result of damage due to infection by other organisms.	
Some organisms reproduce sexually; others, asexually.	

Standards Grid

National Standards: Scientific Inquiry: Grades 5–8	Pages
Many species and plants reproduce sexually. The new individual formed receives genetic materials from both parents but is not identical to those parents.	7, 8, 9, 11, 12, 13
Through heredity, we gain many of our traits. Organisms can be described by their traits, some being environmental and others being inherited.	7, 8, 9, 11, 13
Hereditary information is carried in the genes, which are carried in the chromosomes. Human cells contain many thousands of genes.	7, 8, 9, 11, 13
All organisms must have the ability to live in their constantly changing environment.	19, 22, 33, 34, 35
Behavior can be hereditary (instinctual) or a response built from experience.	14, 41, 42, 43, 52
An organism's behavior is based on that organism's life history.	14, 41, 42, 43
All organisms and their physical surroundings compose an ecosystem.	20, 22, 33, 34, 35, 38
An ecosystem contains producers, consumers, and decomposers. Food webs identify the relationships between these organisms.	20, 22, 33, 34, 35, 44 41, 42, 43, 46, 48
The major source of energy in an ecosystem is sunlight.	41, 42, 43, 45, 47
The number of organisms able to survive in an ecosystem depends on the resources available.	19, 20, 22, 33, 34, 35
Although millions of species of animals, plants, and organisms are alive, there is a unity evident between them—evident through a similarity in structure and internal structure and through common ancestry.	15, 16, 17, 18, 20, 39, 44
Species diversify naturally according to the way they adapt to changes in their surroundings over time.	19, 39, 44
Extinction of species is common and often occurs due to environmental changes.	33, 34, 35, 37

The Father of Genetics—Gregor Mendel

The history of and continuing developments in the study of **genetics** (the study of how parents and offspring have similar and different traits) is filled with complicated and technical information. Many important scientists have contributed their research and knowledge to fill a vast number of books about genetics. But Gregor Mendel, a humble Austrian-born botanist and monk, is the man known as the **"Father of Genetics."**

Born in 1822, Gregor Mendel was considered a brilliant student. He entered the Augustinian monastery in 1843. While in the monastery, he studied science and mathematics, hoping to be a teacher. Although he failed the teacher examination, perhaps because of test-taking stress, Gregor taught at a local high school for about fourteen years.

Mendel also spent time doing scientific experiments. The work he is most recognized for is his work with the simple pea pod plant and the forming of his theories on **heredity**, or the passing on of traits from parent to offspring. Mendel chose the pea plant for several logical reasons. First, the pea plant produces a fairly large number of seeds. Second, this plant can be easily cross-pollinated. And third, the plant has several obvious contrasting characteristics that can be easily studied.

He carefully studied seven traits of the pea plant, including seed shape, seed color, flower position, pod shape, seed coat color, stem length, and pod color. Mendel discovered, after making sure the plants he was using were pure, that crossing two pure plants with the same traits did not guarantee that those traits would show in their offspring. He discovered that if there were different traits in the plants' history, those traits might eventually show.

1. Mendel crossed yellow and green peas.

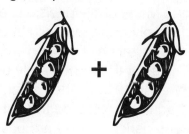

2. Only yellow pea pods were produced.

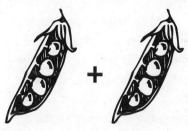

3. When Mendel crossed the yellow offspring, he got both yellow and green.

Because of this research, the terms *recessive traits* and *dominant traits* are part of genetics study. **Recessive traits** are traits that do not show, although they exist in the genes of the offspring. **Dominant traits** are those traits that physically show in the offspring. This theory holds for plants as well as other living things.

The Father of Genetics—Gregor Mendel (cont.)

Mendel presented his findings to a meeting of the Association for Natural Research in 1865. They published the report in a newsletter the following year. Many of his peers believed Mendel had simply done research into successful hybridization. The hard work and findings of the scientist went largely unnoticed until the very early 1900s, when scientists realized he had in fact studied the heredity of certain characteristics as they are passed on from parent to offspring.

Of course, Mendel did not have the technology to find out how the traits are passed on. But his work set the stage for researchers who studied genetics. Simply stated, they discovered threadlike parts, called chromosomes, in the nucleus of each cell. Each chromosome has tiny units all along its length. These are called genes, and they carry the information that determines the traits of an organism. Because of the way cells divide and join during reproduction, offspring end up with half of the mother's chromosomes and half of the father's.

You may ask why this is significant to you. Have you ever wondered why you have the hair or eye color you do? Is it the same or different from that of your parents, brothers, or sisters? This question can be answered using Mendel's theories about dominant and recessive genes. These characteristics are passed on through your genes. A perfect example of the truth in Mendel's research is if you have red hair and the only other person in your family had red hair was a great-great-grandfather. Other traits, such as the ability to roll your tongue, the way your ear lobes are attached to your head, and your skin tone, are passed on through genetic material as well.

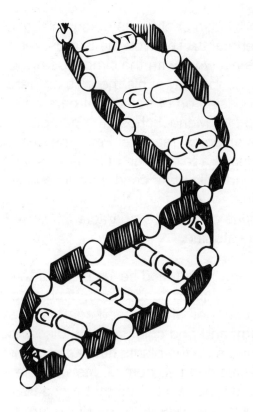

Name_____Date_____

What Do You Remember?

Use the selection on pages 7–8 to answer the following questions.

1. What does the study of genetics involve? _____

   _____

   _____

2. What is meant by the term *dominant trait*? _____

   _____

   _____

3. What is meant by the term *recessive trait*? _____

   _____

   _____

4. What is heredity? _____

   _____

   _____

5. Who is considered the "Father of Genetics"? How did he get the title? _____

   _____

   _____

6. What types of plants did Mendel use to study heredity? Why do you think he used this
   particular plant?

   _____

   _____

   _____

   _____

 0-7424-1917-7 *Write About Life Science*

Name_____ Date_____

Who Is Gregor Mendel?

Fill in the web below using facts about Gregor Mendel's life from the selection on pages 7–8.

Life

Gregor Mendel

Accomplishments

Now use the information from your web to write a paragraph about Mendel. Include your inference on why he might have been so interested in genetics.

_____

_____

_____

_____

_____

_____

_____

_____

_____

Name_____Date_____

Who Are You?

In the space below, sketch a basic family tree. You may trace your own family or interview someone you know. If possible, go back as far as the great-grandparents. Use the family tree to complete the writing activity below.

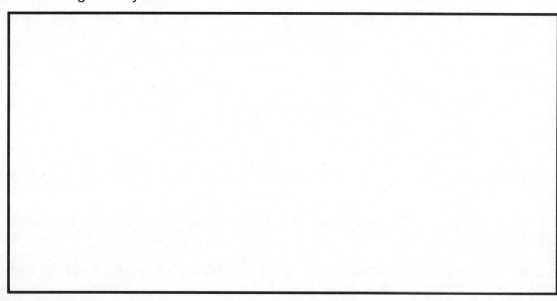

1. Talk about the people in your family or those people that are part of the family tree above. Find out about the physical characteristics and mannerisms that may be similar and passed on from one person to another. Write about the traits that make the people unique to this family. Be sure to write about the people in sequential order.

_____

_____

_____

2. On a sheet of paper, draw a Punnett square like the one to the right. Label it *Female* and *Male,* as shown. Use 12 blue beads as dominant traits and 12 green beads as recessive traits for this activity. Imagine both parents in a family have a gene for blue and a gene for green. Place the beads in the chart to show the probability of that trait showing in offspring. Write about the characteristic found in the offspring of those parents, describing them.

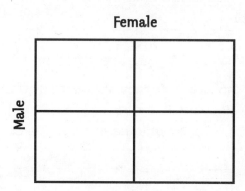

Name_____ Date_____

Boy or Girl

In most animals, including humans, gender is determined by the chromosomes inherited from the parents. If an organism inherits two X chromosomes, it will be female. If the organism inherits an X and a Y chromosome, it will be male.

You can show the chances of having a female or male offspring by doing the activity below.

You Need:
- 2 lima beans
- black permanent marker
- pencil
- paper

Procedure:

1. Mark one lima bean with a Y on one side and an X on the other side. Mark the other bean with an X on both sides.

2. Shake the beans in your hand, and drop them gently to your desk. Record the results on your paper.

3. Repeat step 2 nine more times and record the information. Write your XX results and your XY results over 10, for example, $XX = \frac{6}{10}$

Father										
Mother										

Questions

1. Write about the results of your experiment. Talk about the probability of the offspring being male or female. What factors might have an effect on the results of such an experiment? Are the results guaranteed? Why would people want to know such information?

_____

_____

_____

_____

2. Explain why there is a 50 percent chance that an offspring will be female.

_____

_____

_____

_____

Name_____ Date_____

Inherited Traits

All kinds of traits are inherited: the shape of your nose, the color of your hair, the shape of your body. Many of these traits cannot be changed. Your inherited characteristics are inborn and make you the way you are. Other traits, such as intelligence, personality, and learned abilities, may be inherited to a certain extent but are greatly influenced by your environment and your attitudes toward them. Your mother may have been a talented soccer player and your father a world-class wrestler, but you will not be either unless you choose to put in many long hours of practice.

Which of the following characteristics are inherited? Which of the following characteristics can be changed by your behavior? Mark a U beside the things that cannot be changed and a C beside the things that can be changed.

_____ **1.** your ability to learn spelling words

_____ **2.** the shape of your feet

_____ **3.** your ability to ice skate

_____ **4.** the shape of your teeth

5. Now think about yourself and some of the characteristics you have—things you can change and things you cannot change. Write two paragraphs describing yourself in terms of the characteristics you have thought about.

_____

_____

_____

_____

_____

_____

_____

_____

_____

6. Why do you think it is important to know whether a trait is inherited?

_____

_____

 0-7424-1917-7 *Write About Life Science*

Name_____Date_____

Inherited Behaviors

Inborn, or innate, behavior of an organism is inherited from the parents. The migration of animals and the building of nests are good examples of innate behavior. Inborn behavior includes reflexes and instincts.

Name some inherited behaviors of the animals listed below.

Animals	Inherited Behaviors
Worms	
Spiders	
Insects	
Fish	
Snakes	
Frogs	
Turtles	
Birds	
Cats	
Humans	

1. Choose two of the animals from the list above. Compare and contrast the animals with regard to their inherited behaviors. Hypothesize as to why some of their behaviors are better inherited than learned over time.

Name_____ Date_____

Vertebrates and Invertebrates

The animal kingdom is divided into two main groups—invertebrates and vertebrates. An invertebrate is an animal without a backbone. A vertebrate is an animal with a backbone. Only 4 percent of the approximately 1.5 million known species on Earth are vertebrates. Vertebrates can be divided into five categories, or types. The types are fish, amphibians, reptiles, birds, and mammals. Of the 4 percent of known species that are vertebrates, only a small fraction are mammals.

Look at the table below. Read the basic characteristics and examples of the five basic groups of vertebrates.

Group	Characteristics	Examples
Fish	most often a cold-blooded water creature with an elongated body and fins and gills	sharks and bony fish such as trout, bass, and tuna
Amphibians	most often a cold-blooded creature with young that live in the water and use gills to breathe and adults that are air-breathing	frogs, toads, and salamanders
Reptiles	most often an animal that crawls or moves on the ground on its belly; has a bony skeleton and is covered with scales or bony plates	snakes, lizards, alligators, and turtles
Birds	most often a warm-blooded animal that is covered with feathers, has hollow bones, and has forelimbs modified into wings	robins, ostriches, ducks, and geese
Mammals	most often a warm-blooded animal that feeds its young with milk; has skin and is often covered with hair; gives birth to live young	humans, dogs, whales, platypuses, bats, and apes

While vertebrates are different in many ways, as shown in the table, they also have significant similarities. All of the animals use food to obtain and maintain energy. They all reproduce, give off waste products, and respond to the environment. Vertebrates also are bilaterally symmetrical. This means that the left and right sides of the body are alike. More advanced vertebrates have necks, while others are usually divided into a head and trunk.

Vertebrates and Invertebrates (cont.)

Types of vertebrates are found throughout the world. Certain species are able to survive the polar freeze. Others can live in the tropics. All of these animals have responded to their environment by utilizing the world around them, using available food, water, and shelter. Often animals will change over hundreds of years to adapt to changes that occur in their natural habitat; for example, growing a thicker or thinner coat of fur as abody covering.

Invertebrates are also found throughout the world. They are varied in characteristics. The invertebrates are often categorized into eight different groups. The following chart shows the different types, the characteristics, and examples of each.

Group	Characteristics	Examples
Sponges	vary in shape and size depending on environment; adult sponges live attached to items in the water and never move, they reproduce sexually and asexually	sponges
Cnidarians	hollow-bodied organisms with stinging cells; many have snakelike tentacles that capture food and help them move	coral, jellyfish, and sea anemones
Flatworms	the simplest type of worm; most are parasites; others live in fresh- or saltwater	tapeworms and flukes
Roundworms	found almost everywhere in the world; most are free-living in the soil; more complex than the flatworm; a parasite	nematodes and hookworms
Annelids	most are free-living and live in the soils; some, such as leeches, are parasitic; complex enough to have systems for circulating blood, sensing stimuli, reproduction, and movement	earthworms and leeches
Mollusks	soft bodies generally, but not always, covered with a hard shell; has a special fold of skin called the mantle; a foot aids in movement and capturing prey	clams, squid, and snails
Echinoderms	live in oceans and are covered in spines, which are actually bony plates of the skeleton	sea stars and sand dollars
Arthropods	1 million known species of arthropods on earth; external skeletons, jointed legs	insects, crabs, and crayfish

 0-7424-1917-7 *Write About Life Science*

The Meaning of...

Use the reading selection on pages 15–16 to answer the following.

1. What is a vertebrate? Give three specific examples. _____

_____

2. What is an invertebrate? Give three specific examples. _____

_____

3. What are the five groups of vertebrates? _____

_____

4. What is meant by bilaterally symmetrical? _____

_____

5. Define the word *backbone*. _____

_____

6. Define the word *parasite*. _____

_____

7. What is meant by cold-blooded and warm-blooded? _____

_____

_____

8. What is the mantle on a mollusk? _____

_____

Concept Mapping Invertebrates

Remember that invertebrates are animals that have no backbone. Learn about them by completing a concept map of invertebrates. To complete the map, write one of the subgroups from the box in an empty oval. Then branch off of each subgroup and write group names. An example is done for you. You may want to include sketches.

- sponges
- flatworms
- cnidarians
- arthropods
- mollusks
- roundworms
- segmented worms
- echinoderms

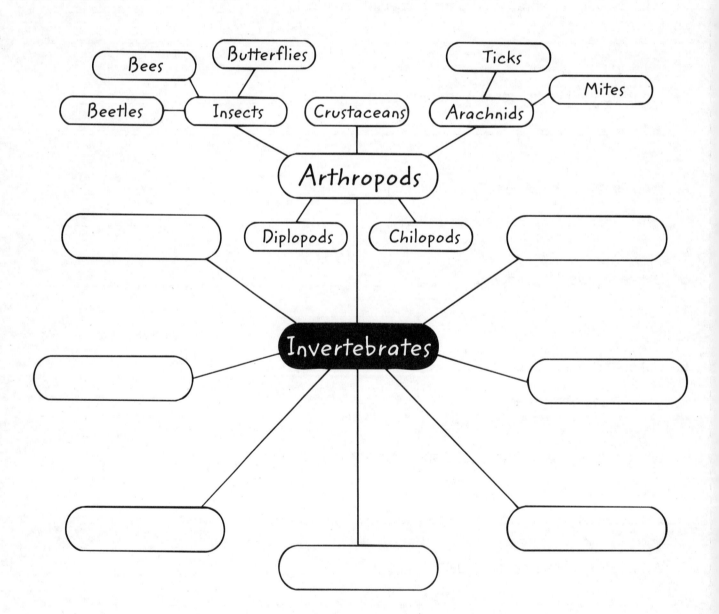

Do the same type of concept map for the vertebrates. Include sketches if possible.

Name_____ Date_____

Animal Adaptations

Animals have adapted to climate changes, changes in food supply, and changes in landforms in order to survive. Choose three of the animals listed below that have had to adapt their lifestyle in order to survive. Research them and write about them.

giant panda	koala	owl	human
chimpanzee	camel	deer	pelican
flying squirrel	sloth	polar bear	giraffe
hummingbird			

1. animal _____

vertebrate or invertebrate _____

special adaptations _____

_____

_____

_____

2. animal _____

vertebrate or invertebrate _____

special adaptations _____

_____

_____

_____

3. animal _____

vertebrate or invertebrate _____

special adaptations _____

_____

_____

_____

Venn Them

Using the information from the reading selection on pages 15–16, complete the Venn diagram below. Compare and contrast characteristics of vertebrates and invertebrates. Be sure to include physical similarities as well as habitats and other habits.

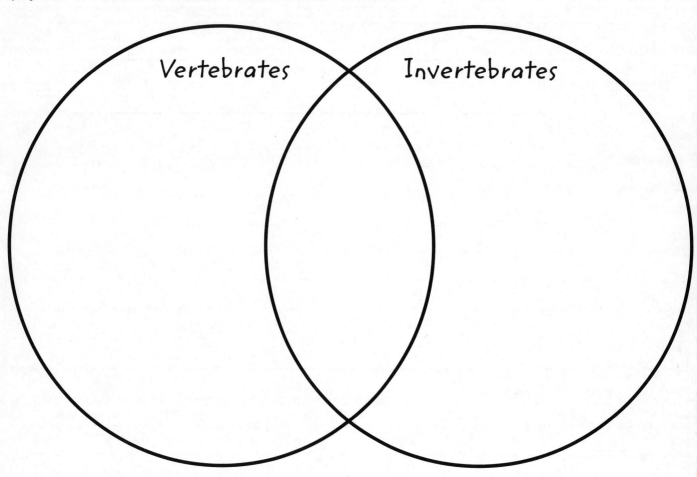

Vertebrates   Invertebrates

Use what you have written in the diagram to write a paragraph about vertebrates and invertebrates. Focus on one aspect of the creatures.

_____

_____

_____

_____

_____

_____

_____

_____

Name_____ Date_____

Earthworm's Soil Conditioning

Earthworms are a very familiar invertebrate to most of us. We can see them in the soil, while out fishing, and as pictures in many books. Earthworms love to dig in the soil. For this activity, you will observe earthworms and their role in the mixing of soil.

You Need:

- one-gallon glass jar
- potting soil
- crushed leaves
- chopped raw potatoes
- builder's sand
- earthworms

Procedure:

1. Obtain live earthworms from a pet store or bait shop.
2. Alternate layers of builder's sand, potting soil, and crushed leaves in the glass jar.
3. Place several earthworms in the glass jar. Add some chopped potatoes.
4. Place the jar in a dark, cool place, or cover it with a cloth.
5. Remove the cloth and observe the conditions in the jar each day. Use the chart below.

Date	Observations

Questions:

1. How has the soil been changed by the earthworms' activities? _____

   _____

2. Of what value are earthworms to the soil in gardens and flower beds? _____

   _____

3. What do you think might happen if the earthworms suddenly disappeared from the soil?

   _____

Name_____ Date_____

Invert Inventory

If you survey a designated area of ground, you may observe many invertebrates you would not usually notice. Conduct a plot survey of an area in the schoolyard, and identify the invertebrates that live or cross that area.

You Need:
- large plastic hoops or string and sticks
- small shovel
- magnifying glass
- 2 data sheets per student (page 23)

Procedure:

1. Select an area of ground you want to study.

2. Place the plastic hoop on the area, or measure off a space, marking it with the string and sticks.

3. Carefully observe your research site.

4. Describe what you see inside your marked area. Is it grassy or all dirt? Is it wet or dry? Is it sunny or shaded? Is it isolated or a heavily used piece of land?

5. Watch for any invertebrates on the surface, and draw them on the data sheet (page 23) as you find them. Use a field guide or another source to help label them.

6. Use the small spade and turn over some ground. Repeat number 5 using a second data sheet.

7. Watch the airspace above the area, and draw and label these invertebrates on a data sheet.

Questions:

1. What factors help determine the types of invertebrates you observe in your area?

_____

2. Describe possible differences in the invertebrates you observe when the seasons change.

_____

3. Would the presence of a vertebrate in the area make a difference in the types of invertebrates you observe? How?

_____

4. What might cause all life in your chosen area to disappear? Explain several possibilities.

_____

Name_____ Date_____

Invert Inventory (cont.)

Invert Inventory Data Sheet

0-7424-1917-7 *Write About Life Science*

Watch the Hatching

Chickens are an example of a familiar vertebrate. You are given a unique opportunity when they are able to observe the hatching of eggs into chicks. You can track the development of the chick from the egg stage all the way to birth and beyond using this long-term project.

You Need:
- incubator
- marker
- sponge
- fertilized eggs
- flashlight
- water

Procedure:

1. Wet a sponge and place it in the incubator for humidity.

2. Carefully mark the eggs with the date they are being put in the incubator.

3. Adjust the incubator to 100°F (68°C).

4. Using the date as a reference point, rotate the eggs a third of a turn each day.

5. At about Day 8, "candle" each egg by placing it in front of the bright flashlight.

6. Check for eyespots, spinal cord, and heart. Draw and write about your observations.

7. After 10 days, dispose of any unfertilized or cracked eggs.

8. Candle the eggs again at Day 17, and draw what you observe.

9. At about Day 21, the eggs will hatch. Note that some chicks may need help emerging from the shells.

Keep track of your observations throughout the experience. Some things you may want to record are these:

- Predictions on whether the chicks will be male or female
- Color of the chicks
- Percentage of eggs that will hatch

Write your thoughts on the following questions.

1. What might happen if the temperature fluctuated during the incubation period?

2. Does it take longer for duck or goose eggs to hatch after fertilization?

3. What might happen if you did not control the moisture level in the air with the wet sponge?

Plant Cell

All living things are made of cells. Some organisms, such as the paramecium and the amoeba, have one cell, while others, such as the human, have millions of cells. Each type of cell has its own function. Plant cells have different functions than human muscle cells, for example. Look at the diagrams below and on the next page. They show similarities and differences between a plant cell and an animal cell. Be sure to read the descriptions of the parts of the cell.

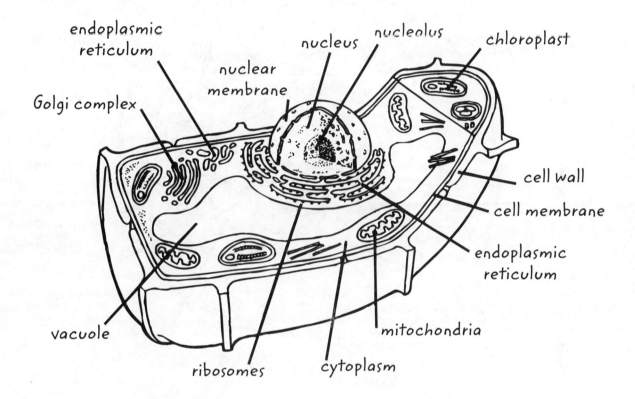

ribosomes—where proteins are made
Golgi complex—stores and releases chemicals
cytoplasm—jellylike substance within the cell
nucleus—chromosomes are found here
nucleolus—spherical body within the nucleus
nuclear membrane—holds nucleus together
mitochondria—releases energy from the nutrients
cell wall—shapes and supports a plant cell
vacuole—contains water and dissolved minerals
chloroplast—food for plant cells is made here
cell membrane—controls entry into and out of the cell
endoplasmic reticulum—surface for chemical activity

Each small part of the cell is called an organelle. Each organelle has its own name and function. Many of the organelles in a plant cell are also in an animal cell.

Name_____ Date_____

Animal Cell

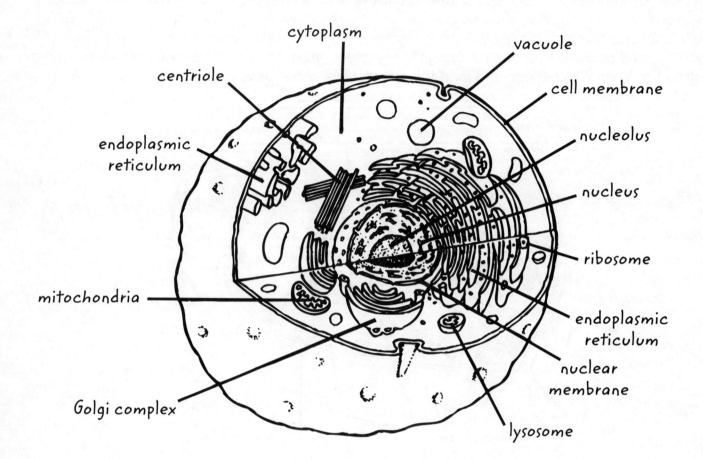

vacuole—contains water and dissolved minerals

lysosome—digests large particles

ribosomes—where proteins are made

Golgi complex—stores and releases chemicals

cytoplasm—jellylike substance within the cell

nucleus—chromosomes are found here

nucleolus—spherical body within the nucleus

nuclear membrane—holds nucleus together

cell membrane—controls entry into and out of the cell

mitochondria—releases energy from the nutrients

endoplasmic reticulum—surface for chemical activity

centriole—structures involved in mitosis in animal cells only

Name_____ Date_____

Definitely Cellular

Use the reading selection and the diagrams on pages 25–26 to define the following terms.

1. ribosomes _____

_____

2. cytoplasm _____

_____

3. nucleus _____

_____

4. nuclear membrane _____

_____

5. mitochondria _____

_____

6. cell membrane _____

_____

7. Golgi complex _____

_____

8. vacuole _____

_____

Now use the words above to complete the following sentences.

9. The _____ holds the cell together.

10. The _____, organelles specific to green plants, contain the chemical chlorophyll, which permits a green plant to produce its own sugar.

Name_____Date_____

What's the Difference?

Look at the diagrams and descriptions of the animal and plant cells on pages 25–26.

1. Write about the differences that are obvious between the two cells. Think about why many parts are the same, and write about why you think that might be.

   _____

   _____

   _____

   _____

2. What might plants be like if their cells had no chloroplast? How might it make a difference?

   _____

   _____

   _____

   _____

3. Why do you think plant cells have cell walls instead of cell membranes? Why do you think animal cells have cell membranes instead of cell walls?

   _____

   _____

   _____

   _____

4. Do you think plant or animal cells use more energy to live? Why?

   _____

   _____

   _____

   _____

Name_____Date_____

What Do You See?

Do the following experiment to see examples of a typical plant cell. Then write about what you see.

You Need:

- eye dropper
- tap water
- microscope

- microscope slide and cover
- sample of *Elodea* (common waterweed)
- red onion skin also works well

Procedure:

1. Create a chart like the one to the right.

2. Put two drops of water on a microscope slide.

3. Tear a leaf from the waterweed, and place it in the water on the slide. Make sure it is lying flat.

4. Cover the leaf with the cover.

5. Place the slide under the microscope.

Cell under low power	Cell under high power

Observations:

1. Look closely at the leaf under the low power. Draw your observations and label the cell parts you can see.

2. Now look at the leaf under high power. Draw what you observe.

3. Write about the differences between the two views of the cell.

_____

_____

_____

Name_____ Date_____

Very Cheeky

Do the following experiment to observe human cheek cells. Then compare the cheek cell with the plant cell observed on page 29.

You Need:
- compound microscope
- methylene blue stain
- 2 glass slides
- 2 cover slips
- eye dropper
- toothpick (flat type)
- water

Procedure:

1. Put a drop of stain on a slide, being careful as it will stain skin and clothing. Gently scrape the inside of your cheek with a toothpick. **CAUTION:** *Do not scrape hard enough to injure your cheek.*

2. Rub the toothpick in the stain. Break the toothpick in half and discard.

3. Cover the slide with a cover slip.

4. Locate the nucleus, cytoplasm, and cell membrane. Fill in the table below by putting a check mark in the box if the cell part can be seen.

5. Draw and label the nucleus, cytoplasm, and cell membrane of a cheek cell.

6. Refer back to the work done with the waterweed. Fill in the chart with the information about the *Elodea* cell.
   NOTE: Lifting cells from a washed wrist by placing clear tape on the skin also works well.

Cell Parts	Cheek cell parts present	Elodea cell parts present
Cytoplasm		
Nucleus		
Chloroplast		
Cell wall		
Cell membrane		

1. Describe the shape of a cheek cell. Compare it to the shape and look of the waterweed cell.

_____

2. Name the parts found in plant cells that are absent in animal cells.

_____

3. Why do you think stains such as methylene blue are used when observing cells under the microscope?

_____

4. Why don't animal cells have chloroplasts?

_____

Name_____ Date_____

Make a Cell

Create a cell.

You Need:

- lemon gelatin
- grapes (cut in half)
- lettuce
- gallon-sized resealable bags
- bowl
- shredded carrots
- raisins
- other assorted vegetables and fruits
- cake pan
- markers or small paper flags for labeling

On the lines below, describe how you built your cell. Write the directions in sequential order, numbering them. Be sure to include what each item represents in the cell; for example, the carrot shreds may stand for the mitochondria. When labeling, be sure to identify your cell as a plant or animal cell.

_____

_____

_____

_____

_____

_____

_____

_____

_____

_____

_____

_____

_____

_____

_____

_____

_____

_____

Name_____ Date_____

A Special Science Tool

The microscope is a necessary tool when observing tiny organisms in life science. In about 1590, two Dutch spectacle makers, Hans and Zaccharias Janssen, started experimenting with lenses. They put several lenses in a tube and made a very important discovery. The object near the end of the tube appeared to be greatly enlarged! They had just invented the compound microscope.

Other people heard of the Janssen's work and started work of their own. Galileo added a focusing device. Anthony Leeuwenhoek of Holland became so interested that he learned how to make lenses. By grinding and polishing, he was able to make small lenses with great curvatures. These rounder lenses produced greater magnification, and his microscopes were able to magnify up to 270 times.

Anthony Leeuwenhoek's new, improved microscope allowed people to see things no human had ever seen before. He saw bacteria, yeast, and blood cells. Because of his great contributions, he has been called the "Father of Microscopy."

Robert Hooke, an Englishman, also spent much of his life working with microscopes and improved their design and capabilities. He coined the word *cell* after observing cork cells under a microscope. He was reminded of a monk's cell in a monastery.

Little was done to improve the microscope until the middle of the 19th century, when great strides were made and quality instruments such as today's microscope emerged.

Use the words from the Word Bank and a science resource book to help you label this microscope.

WORD BANK
- eyepiece
- fine adjustment
- stage
- mirror
- body tube
- objective
- stage clips
- diaphragm
- coarse adjustment
- arm
- base
- nosepiece

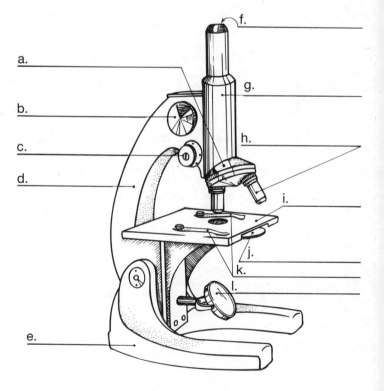

A Closer Look

As a freelance writer and naturalist, I have accepted many exciting assignments all over the world. My love and respect for the great outdoors and all of nature has landed me some really amazing writing assignments, from a photographic safari of the Serengeti Plains to the stalking of walruses of the Arctic. But certainly one of the most rewarding was a hike through the wilds of Alaska, observing the big brown bear, or grizzly bear.

My research told me that the largest population of this species of bear, the *ursus arctos horribilis*, could be found along the coastlands of Alaska. So my photographer and I packed our bags, gathered supplies, and chartered a floatplane to that glorious state. We landed in a remote inlet on the southeastern coast and unloaded our supplies. We arranged to meet the pilot in the same spot in 15 days and waved him off.

I was in awe of the scenery. In no other place did I feel so at peace with my surroundings. There was something about this part of the country that always made me take stock of myself and what my job was—to teach others respect and responsibility for nature through my writing. Phil and I hoisted our packs onto our shoulders and walked to a small building that had housed a remote radio station. Tucked inside an old frame hanging askew on the wall, a map of the state of Alaska greeted us. There were notes and arrows all over it. "Stay away from the ledge," warned one. Other notes said things such as, "Saw grizzly pack here" and "Best view."

Phil and I knew our way around this area, as we had been here last year covering an assignment about humpback whales and some unusually heavy activity in the area. We nodded at each other. He pointed to a spot on the map, Pack Creek in the Stan Price State Wildlife Sanctuary, and we started out.

It wasn't long before we encountered our first wildlife. A lone grizzly ambled through the woods in the same direction Phil and I were moving. Blond in color instead of dark brown, he was a fairly large bear, perhaps 700 pounds and seven and a half feet tall. The male grizzly can grow to be as large as 1,100 pounds and seven to nine feet tall, so he was an average-sized bear. Phil and I watched as he swung his body to a standing position next to a tree and reached for some berries, a favorite food of the large omnivore.

We veered to the south and continued on to Pack Creek. We were sure to see some great specimens there since the salmon were running. The salmon run brought grizzlies from all around the sanctuary, sometimes gathering in groups of ten or more, to catch the fish. It is an amazing sight to see these expert fishers literally grab fish from the loud rushing water using their long claws, or almost effortlessly pounce on the unsuspecting chum salmon and smack it into the riverbed, killing it. With approximately 2.4 bears per square mile in the area, we were sure to see more as we hiked our way through the sanctuary land.

A Closer Look (cont.)

We were glad we had chosen the Stan Price State Wildlife Sanctuary as our destination. The grizzly, also known as a brown bear, enjoys solitude and dense forests to populated and open spaces. And with the salmon running, the more popular places for grizzly sightings here, such as McNeil River Falls, were sure to have the limit of wildlife watchers. On a good day, spectators could see more than thirty bears feeding at the falls at one time. As we approached Pack Creek, Phil and I could hear the rush of water. Spreading the branches of a creekside clump of brush, Phil almost dropped his camera. He was staring into the broad brown face of a grizzly. The unmistakable hump of muscle mass on his shoulders and the white-tipped hairs that gave him a grizzled appearance left no doubt that this was a grizzly.

Of course, Phil and I handled the situation like experts. We didn't run, the first rule of thumb when that close to a bear. We eased our way out of the brush and waited. The grizzly eventually went back to the creekside and the salmon. As we took the opportunity to get further away, we found a great vantage point from some low-hanging branches and snapped spectacular pictures.

We set up camp later that day and talked about the grizzly. Phil didn't know as much as I about the bear, so I filled him in. He was especially interested in the bear population. We discussed the fact that grizzlies are considered a threatened species, with approximately 850 bears in the lower 48 states and perhaps over 30,000 in Alaska. Logging, mining, and human development, as well as illegal poaching, are the major threats to this species.

I had made the observation that the bears at Pack Creek all seemed to be older males. Phil found that interesting too. He mentioned he had read about the fact that many females travel with their young for typically up to two years. The female is fiercely protective of her offspring during this time. She teaches them survival skills, including hunting for food and defending themselves, although it is well known that, except for humans, grizzlies are not prey for any creature. After about two years, the bears will set off on their own and the mother bears may then have another litter of cubs, which is typically two.

As the sun set on that third day, we recapped our observations. I then headed for my tent to dictate notes into my cassette recorder. Phil said he would make sure the food was secured for the night, putting leftover fruit in the airtight containers we had brought. As I zipped up the flap of my tent, I wondered what another day at Pack Creek would bring.

Read All About It

1. sanctuary _____

_____

2. offspring _____

_____

3. litter _____

_____

4. grizzled _____

_____

5. species _____

_____

6. endangered species _____

_____

7. poach _____

_____

8. omnivore _____

_____

Recall facts from the story to answer the following questions.

9. What is the size of an average-sized grizzly bear? _____

10. Name four factors from the story that are major threats to the grizzly bear becoming extinct. What are two other factors that may make a difference in the bear's survival?

_____

_____

11. Why do you think it is a common rule of thumb not to run when confronted with a grizzly bear?_____

_____

12. Why do you think the men had to place their leftover food in airtight containers for the night?

_____

_____

A Mammal Too

The grizzly bear is a mammal. A mammal is a vertebrate animal that has hair (or fur) and feeds its young milk. Think about other mammals besides the bear. Some very familiar ones include the dog, cat, tiger, lion, and zebra.

Choose any three mammals. Compare and contrast the three animals using the Venn diagram below. Then take that information and write at least two paragraphs about the mammals you chose.

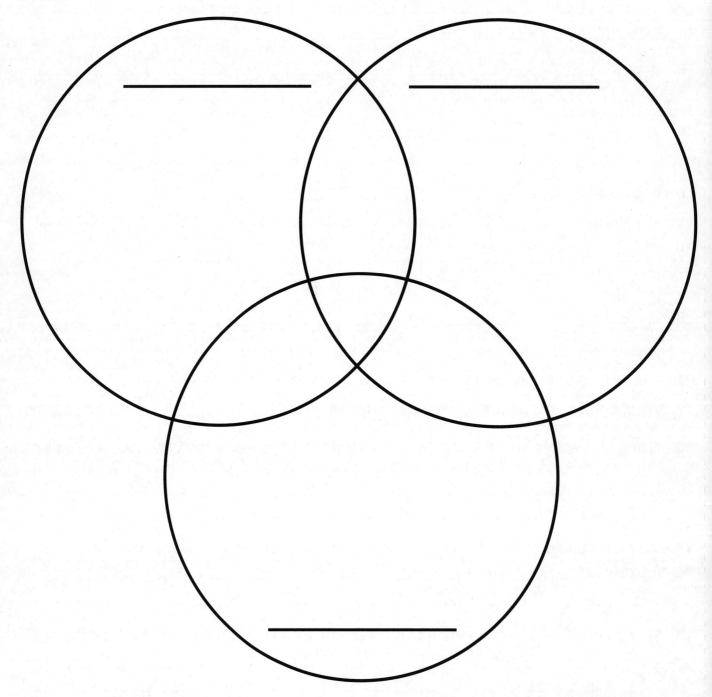

Name_____ Date_____

Predicting the Future

Many species of animals have become endangered. This means that due to forces beyond the animals' control, they are becoming extinct, or dying. Reasons for animals becoming endangered include, but are not exclusive to, depletion of the food supply, legal or illegal hunting of bears, and the disappearance or pollution of their habitat.

Brown (or grizzly) bears are considered an endangered species in the continental United States. In the space below, write about the grizzly. Tell why you think it has become part of the group of endangered species. Predict the future of the bear. Tell what you think might happen if the conditions do not improve for the grizzly. Include several solutions to the bear's dilemma.

_____

_____

_____

_____

_____

_____

_____

_____

_____

_____

_____

_____

_____

_____

_____

_____

How does the endangerment and extinction of certain species have an effect on your life?

_____

_____

Name_____Date_____

Home Sweet Home

Just like most living creatures, grizzly bears need to live where they have their needs met and can survive and reproduce. The bears' habitat must have food and water available to sustain them throughout the year. They need to stay healthy and strong so they can raise their young and continue to find food.

Reread the passages on pages 33–34 describing a grizzly bear habitat. In outline form, list the details of the habitat, including food sources and other characteristics of the habitat. Extend the outline using your own knowledge and theories. Add details about other wildlife that may be present in the habitat. Include characteristics of the overall climate. Add other information about the ideal grizzly bear habitat.

   I. Grizzly Habitat
      A. Food Sources
         1. _____
         2. _____
         3. _____
      B. Surrounding Nature
         1. _____
         2. _____
         3. _____
         4. _____
      C. Other Wildlife
         1. _____
         2. _____
         3. _____
      D. Ideal Climate
         1. _____
         2. _____

II. _____
      A. _____
         1. _____
         2. _____
      B. _____
         1. _____
         2. _____

Consider the ideal habitat for the grizzly bear. How have humans and their influence made it difficult for the grizzly?

_____

_____

Name_____ Date_____

Family Tree

Many species of bears belong to the ursus family tree. While various species have many similarities, there are also obvious differences—from where they live, the climate they most enjoy, and the foods they eat.

Choose three different species of bears, and complete the charts below. Use research sources if necessary. Answer in complete sentences.

Name of Bear: _____

Habits: _____

Habitat: _____

Food: _____

Color/Size: _____

Fun Facts: _____

Name of Bear: _____

Habits: _____

Habitat: _____

Food: _____

Color/Size: _____

Fun Facts: _____

Name of Bear: _____

Habits: _____

Habitat: _____

Food: _____

Color/Size: _____

Fun Facts: _____

Now use the information you have written to compose an essay about the ursus family tree. Include your theories as to why there are so many different species, how they came to be located all over the world, and how most species have managed to survive in such a changing world.

Name_____ Date_____

The Next Few Days

Continue the story begun on pages 33–34. Use the words in the Word Bank. Be sure to use facts about the brown bear as you write about the further adventures of the author and his photographer.

Word Bank

carnivore	herbivore	omnivore	paws
bellow	climb	den	cubs
riverbed	species	habitat	conservation
endangered	humans		

_____

_____

_____

_____

_____

_____

_____

_____

_____

_____

_____

_____

_____

_____

_____

_____

_____

_____

_____

_____

_____

_____

Food Chains and Food Webs

The whole ecology of a given location on the earth can become unbalanced with the disappearance of just a single creature. This is because of a system called the food chain. The *food chain* is a concept that was developed by a scientist named Charles Elton. In 1927, he laid out the process by which plants get their energy from the sunlight, plant-eating animals get their energy from eating plants, and meat-eating animals get their energy from other animals. Seen in black and white, this looks very much like a chain, with its links all together.

Let's look at the food chain more closely. The food chain has four basic parts.

• The first part is the *sun*. The sun provides the energy for everything on the earth.

• The second part is known as *producers*. Producers are all green plants. They make their own food, and every organism is in part dependent on plants for the oxygen and/or food they need.

• *Consumers* are the third part of the food chain. Consumers are, very simply, every organism that eats something else, whether it is a carnivore (eats meat), a herbivore (eats plants), an omnivore (eats plants and animals), a parasite (relies on another living thing to provide food), or a scavenger (usually feeds on dead orgnisms).

• The fourth part of the food chain is *decomposers*. These organisms, such as fungi and bacteria, break down dead matter into important gases that are released back into the ground, air, or water. These "recycled" nutrients are then used by the producers in their growth process.

Look at the simplified food chain below. The sunlight helps the grass to grow, the rabbit eats the grass, and the fox eats the rabbit. Because the fox does not have a predator, it is the "top" of this food chain.

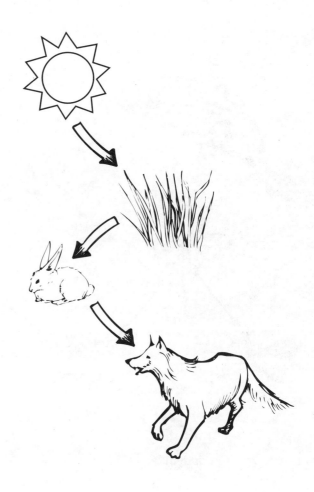

If something happens to the grass—perhaps a drought occurs—and the rabbits have less food, many may die. Without as many rabbits to eat, some of the foxes in the area may also die or leave the location. While this is a very simple look at the food chain (because rabbits do eat things other than grass), you can see that the disappearance of one element in the chain can have a lasting effect.

Food Chains and Food Webs (cont.)

The term *food web* describes the many interlocking food chains in an area somewhere on the earth or in the water. Look at the food web below. Notice how the crops are eaten by humans, birds, aphids, and crickets or how the cricket is eaten by the chameleon and the frog. This shows very clearly how one food chain relies on another. It also shows how the failing of one element in a food chain might affect all living things in a location.

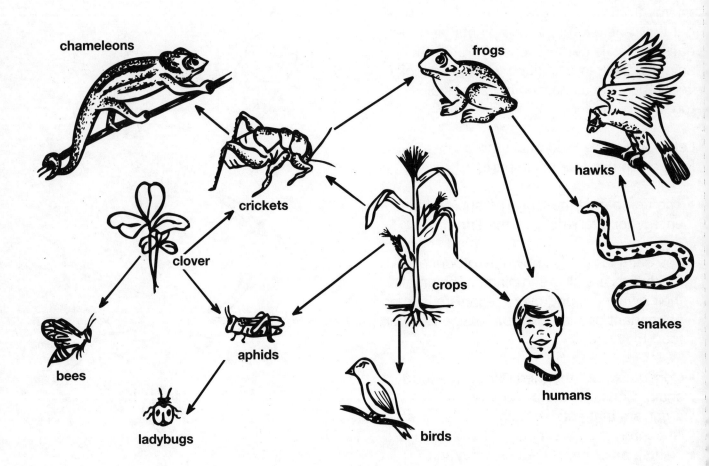

By breaking one link in an existing food chain, we run the risk of threatening all of the organisms above that one link, as well as other chains in a large food web. And this has happened many times. One example is the use of the pesticide DDT in the 1960s. This pesticide was very effective in helping to eliminate certain insects. But as it washed off the plants and out of the soil into the water supply, plankton and other small organisms took in the DDT. These organisms were then eaten by small fish, resulting in the fish having the DDT in them. Larger fish and birds ate the smaller fish, and the birds were affected. Birds such as the osprey and eagle developed very thin eggshells and became threatened. This is known as the "domino effect."

Look Closer

Use the reading on pages 41–42 to help define the following terms.

1. consumers _____

_____

2. producers _____

_____

3. sun _____

_____

4. pesticides _____

_____

5. food chain _____

_____

6. food web _____

_____

7. domino effect _____

_____

8. energy _____

_____

Now answer the following questions.

9. What term means that the "death of one species in a food chain upsets the rest of the food chain"? _____

_____

10. Look at the food web on page 42. Describe several different food chains in the web.

_____

_____

Chain Reactions Everywhere

All organisms need food and energy whether they are in or above the water. Energy comes from many sources, and those sources are usually a part of a food chain. In the spaces below, create one marine food chain and one land food chain. Make sure the "links" in the chains are in sequential order.

Marine Food Chain

Land Food Chain

Consider the food chains you have recorded. Would a marine food web have as many elements in it as a land food web? Why or why not?

_____

_____

_____

_____

_____

_____

Your Daily Menu

We eat food from many sources. We eat fruits, vegetables, meats, dairy, grains, and sweets. Most items that are part of our daily diet are made from natural source such as potatoes, cows, and wheat plants. Each of those items needed energy to grow and mature so that they were ready to be producers or sources of the foods we eat.

For example, wheat plants get their energy to grow from the sun and the nutrients in the soil and water. Cows get their energy from the plants and grains they are fed. Those plants and grains grow like the wheat plant does, and they are all part of a food web.

Choose three of your favorite foods. Write the ingredients of the food, and trace a food chain to show where those ingredients came from.

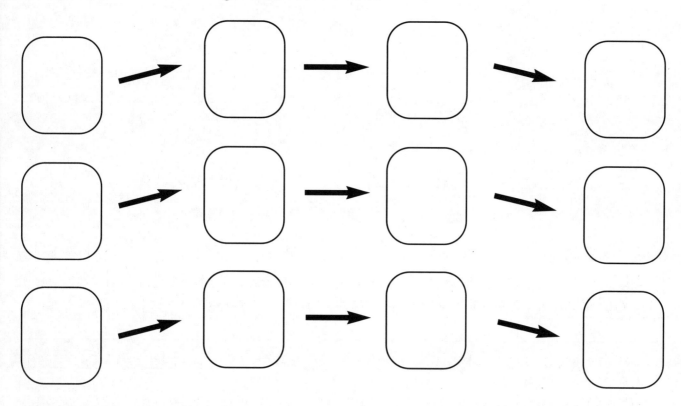

Is there an item in your diet that isn't made from something that grows naturally? Name it and explain where it comes from.

_____

_____

_____

_____

Name_____Date_____

Shop Around

What happens when one organism in a food chain simply dies, becomes extinct, or leaves an area? How are the rest of the organisms in the food chain and food web affected? What types of repercussions might there be if two organisms disappear from a food chain or web?

These are the types of questions that some researchers and scientists must ask themselves. As the world changes and the atmosphere is affected by changes in the ozone layer and by the weather patterns on Earth, this is what happens.

Study the food chain shown below, and answer the questions that follow.

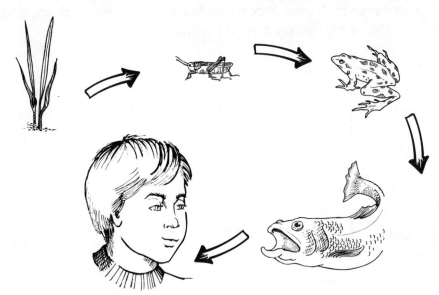

1. Predict what might happen if the stream that the fish and frogs live in and around began to dry up. What effect might this have on the food web in the area?

   _____

   _____

2. If a large group of foxes came into the area and began eating the frog population, what might happen?

   _____

   _____

3. Create a new food chain showing how things might change if the frog and fish populations were depleted. Consider what might replace them in the chain and how it might have an effect on the larger food web. After drawing and labeling the new chain, write about the changes that would take place.

Name_____ Date_____

Energy Pyramid

An energy pyramid is a way of describing the feeding and energy relationships within a food chain or web. Each step in an energy pyramid shows that some energy is stored in newly made structures of the organism that eats the one before it. The pyramid also shows that much of the energy is lost when one organism in a food chain eats another. Most of this lost energy goes into the environment as heat energy. While a continuous input of energy from sunlight keeps the process going, the height of energy pyramids (and therefore the length of food chains) is limited by this loss of energy.

The picture is an energy pyramid. Producer organisms represent the greatest amount of living tissue, or biomass, at the bottom of the pyramid. The organisms that occupy the rest of the pyramid belong to the feeding levels shown in the diagram. On average, each feeding level contains 10 percent of the energy as the one below it, with the energy that is lost being changed mostly to heat.

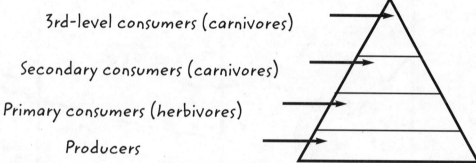

3rd-level consumers (carnivores)

Secondary consumers (carnivores)

Primary consumers (herbivores)

Producers

Answer the following questions using the information above.

1. Define the following:

   a. carnivore _____

   b. herbivore _____

   c. biomass _____

2. Explain the difference between a food chain and an energy pyramid.

   _____

3. Are there similarities between what we call a food pyramid and the energy pyramid?

   _____

4. Construct an energy pyramid showing the different feeding levels and naming specific organisms.

Name_____Date_____

Food for Thought

| Producers | First-Order Consumers | Second-Order Consumers | Third-Order Consumers |

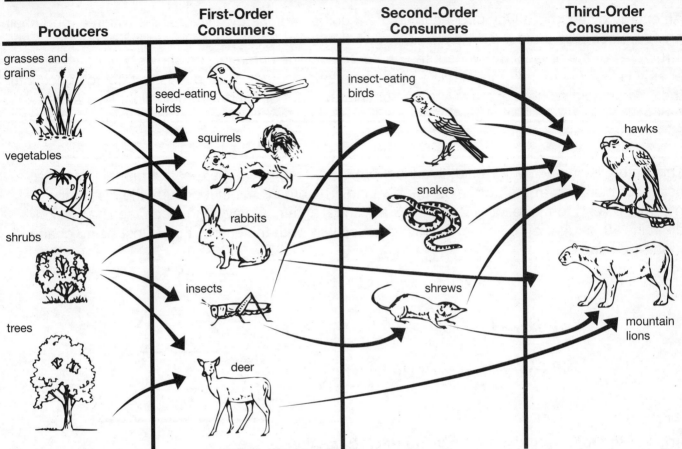

Use the food web to answer the following questions.

1. When the hawk is the third-order consumer, the number of second-order consumers is

   _____.

2. The food chain that includes insect-eating birds is

   _____.

3. The animal that consumes the largest number of different types of first-order and second-order consumers is the

   _____.

4. All of the animals that are herbivores are

   _____.

5. If there were no snakes in this web, the squirrels and rabbits could still be eaten by the

   _____.

Name_____ Date_____

That's Nervy

The human nervous system is what enables you to sense, analyze, and respond to what is going on around you as well as inside your body. Without the ability to be aware of the changes going on, you and your body could suffer some irreversible consequences. This complex system that includes the nerves, brain, spinal cord, and certain glands are all in tune with one another to help ensure health, emotional well-being, and safety.

The nervous system is really two major parts. The **central nervous system** is the brain and spinal cord. The **peripheral nervous system** includes the nerves that branch off of the brain and spinal cord. These nerves connect almost every part of your body to the central nervous system and can extend from the tips of your toes to your scalp. They carry messages from one area of the body to another. These messages, called **impulses**, can travel as fast as 100 meters per second. The nerve cells that send these impulses use electrical signals to transmit them.

Each nerve cell has three main components—a cell body, an axon, and many dendrites. The **cell body** contains the nucleus and controls the activity of the rest of the cell. The **axon** relays information from one cell to another. The **dendrites**, which resemble tiny branches on a tree, receive information from the other nerve cells or from the environment that is demanding a response. The information is transferred across small spaces between the axon of one nerve cell and the dendrites of the next. This space is called the **synapse**. When the impulse reaches the tip of one axon, a chemical is released. This chemical helps the impulse to travel between the two nerve cells and on to the next.

There are three types of nerve cells in the human body, each with its own job. One kind of cell is the **sensory nerve cell**. This cell receives information from the surroundings and transmits it to the brain and spinal cord. The messages are from special cells called sensory receptors. The sense organs, such as the eyes and nose, contain these receptors. They help detect light, smells, and sounds. In other areas of the body, they detect heat, touch, pain, and pressure.

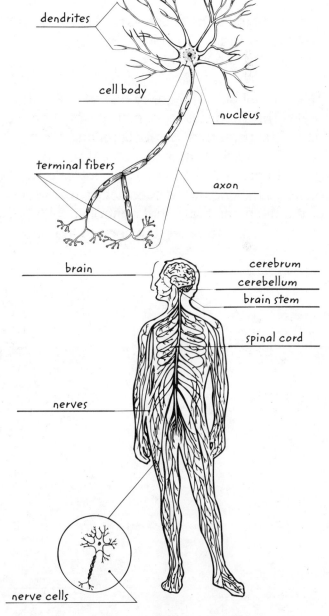

That's Nervy (cont.)

Another type of nerve cell is the **motor nerve cell**. This cell sends the information from the brain and spinal cord to muscles and glands, which determines the action of the muscles and glands. These cells cause the voluntary muscles in your body to move, allowing you to hop, skip, run, and walk. These motor nerve cells also help the involuntary muscles do things such as control breathing and control the actions of the body's systems, such as the digestive system.

The third type of cells are **association nerve cells** in the brain and spinal cord. They connect the other two types of cells.

The cells all ultimately send messages to the brain. The brain has three main components or parts: the cerebrum, cerebellum, and brain stem. The **cerebrum** is the largest part of the brain. In general, it controls thinking and decision making. More specifically, this section of the brain has areas that control speech, sight, touch, and other functions of the body.

The **cerebellum** has small spaces between the axon of one nerve cell and the dendrites of the next. It carries out the activity the cerebrum decides the body should do. Whenever your body is in motion, doing something such as exercising, the cerebellum is at work.

The **brain stem** is located between the cerebrum and the spinal cord. This part of the brain helps sort messages and transfers them where they need to be. It has another important part to it, the medulla. The medulla has the important task of controlling automatic activity such as blood pressure and heart rate. Deep inside the brain and right above the brain stem is another part of the brain called the hypothalamus. This part of the brain regulates digestion and body temperature.

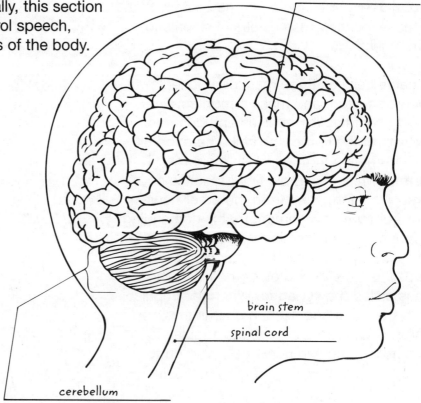

cerebrum

brain stem

spinal cord

cerebellum

Name_____ Date_____

Don't Be Nervous

Use the reading selection on pages 49–50 to help you define the following words.

1. cerebrum _____
_____

2. cerebellum _____
_____

3. hypothalamus _____
_____

4. medulla _____
_____

5. central nervous system _____
_____

6. peripheral nervous system _____
_____

7. impulses _____
_____

8. axon _____
_____

9. dendrite _____
_____

10. synapse _____
_____

Use your own words to describe the work of the following nerve cells.

11. sensory nerve cells _____
_____

12. association nerve cells _____
_____

13. motor nerve cells _____
_____

Right or Left

The cerebrum is divided into two hemispheres, or halves, of brain. The right hemisphere controls most of the actions of the left side of the body. It also deals more with visual activities and plays a role in putting things together. For example, it takes visual information, puts it together, and says "I recognize that—that's a pear" or "That's a dog" or "That's a house." It organizes or groups information together.

The left side of the brain controls most of the actions of the right side of the body. This hemisphere tends to be the more analytical half; it analyzes information collected by the right side. It takes information from the right hemisphere and applies language to it. The right hemisphere "sees" a house, but the left hemisphere says, "I know whose house that is—it's Uncle Bob's house."

Think about the jobs that each side of the brain has. Read each statement below and indicate whether it is a right-brain function or a left-brain function. Write R if it is right and L if it is left.

_____ **1.** I am working a simple addition problem in math.

_____ **2.** Tanya remembered the three new phone numbers.

_____ **3.** Mika gave her opinion of the new song.

_____ **4.** We painted the bathroom blue.

_____ **5.** Ms. Paulie said to outline the article.

_____ **6.** Grandma organized her entire closet into little plastic boxes.

Now answer these questions.

7. Think about the work you do at school. List some of the tasks that would be considered a right-brain function. Compare them to several activities that you consider left-brain activities. Which tasks feel easier and more rewarding to you? Why do you think that is so?

_____

_____

_____

8. What do you think would happen if everyone was right-brain dominant, meaning that all people would think more globally and would be more creative?

_____

_____

Name_____Date_____

Find Your Brain Dominance

Remember that the cerebellum controls all voluntary movement. These actions include walking, running, and writing. One side of the brain is usually dominant, or depended upon more heavily. The side that is most dominant depends on the individual. The left side is controlled by the right side of the brain, and the right side is controlled by the left side. This means that a person who writes with his right hand is probably left-brain dominant.

Do the activities in the chart, and checking Right or Left after each task. Then answer the questions below to help determine whether you are right- or left-brain dominant.

Try This:	Right	Left
Clasp your hands together. Which hand is on top?		
Pick up a pencil to write. Which hand do you use?		
Take 3 steps. Which leg is in front?		
Try to do the splits. Which leg is in front?		
Cross your arms. Which arm is on top?		
Wink your eye. Which one did you wink?		
Pick up a fork. Which hand do you eat with?		
Hop 5 times. Which foot did you use?		
Look through a camera, telescope, or microscope. Which eye did you use?		

1. How many times did you use your right? _____

2. How many times did you use your left? _____

3. Which side of your brain is probably more dominant? _____

4. What might happen if one side of your brain could not function at its fullest potential? How might this have an effect on the things you do?

    _____

    _____

5. Do you think you could "train" yourself to be more dominant on the side opposite of what was indicated in the test above? How might you do that? Give specific examples.

    _____

    _____

Name_____ Date_____

Imagine This

We rely on our senses everyday. We develop certain senses, such as our smell, sight, and hearing, to a level of sensitivity that helps us live our daily lives smoothly and without too many difficulties. But there are times when the sensory nerve cells do not work to their full capacity. Perhaps the cells suffered some damage or the area of the brain that controls a particular sense suffered a trauma. In this case, a person must compensate for the loss of the sense. She must work to sharpen other senses that can take the place of the missing sense or work to overcome any difficulties that may have resulted because of the loss.

Imagine you have lost the sense of sight. To help you get a stronger idea of what this might be like, wear a blindfold during a class presentation or video. After the presentation is done, ask yourself the following questions.

1. Specifically, what was I unable to do? _____

2. What did I do to compensate for the "loss" of sight? _____

3. As a result of a loss of sight, what other sense or senses might develop more fully to compensate? Why?

   _____

   _____

4. Have you ever observed someone who is challenged by a loss of sight? What types of things did that person use to help make up for the loss? What tools or special actions seemed to help?

   _____

   _____

5. Now do the same activity, this time using one of the other senses. You could use earplugs, a swimmer's nose plug, or heavy gloves to help you simulate the experience. Write about the new experience on the lines below.

   _____

   _____

   _____

   _____

   _____

Name_____ Date_____

It's a Reflex Action

Observe some reflexes. Remember that reflexes are automatic responses to an event, spurred on by the nervous system. The message does not travel to the brain first. Your body reacts and then the brain registers any information it needs.

Observe the knee jerk reflex and the blinking reflex.

You Need:
- clear transparency plastic   • popped popcorn   • a partner

Procedure (blinking reflex):

1. Have your partner hold the transparency in front of his face.
2. Gently, without preparing him, toss a piece of popcorn at the plastic sheet.
3. Observe him eyes' reaction to the popcorn hitting the plastic.
4. Record the results in a chart similar to the one below. Repeat steps 2 and 3 four more times.

Procedure (knee jerk):

1. Relax and sit in a chair with your legs crossed and your eyes closed.
2. With the side of his hand, have your partner lightly but firmly tap your leg under the kneecap.
3. Observe the action that takes place, and record the results in the chart.
4. Repeat steps 2 and 3 four more times.

		Blinking Reflex	Knee Jerk Reflex
	1st Try		
	2nd Try		
	3rd Try		
	4th Try		
	5th Try		

Now answer the following.

1. Did the results of the two experiments vary from try to try? How? Why would this happen?

_____

_____

2. Blinking is a protective reflex action. What are some other protective reflexes that your nervous system provides your body? If you could program yourself to respond reflexively to other stimuli, what would those reflexes be?

_____

Name_____Date_____

Map Your Tongue

The human tongue is a sense organ that has a very high nerve cell density. It is uniquely suited to taste, but not all of the nerve cells sense the same taste. Some recognize sweet, some identify sour, and others sense saltiness. Because of this, there are "regions" on the tongue.

Do the following experiment with a partner to locate the taste regions on your tongue.

You Need:
- cotton swabs
- small piece of paper
- lemon juice
- cups of water
- sugar
- salt
- measuring spoons

Procedure:

1. Prepare three paper cups for the taste test.

2. Add 3 mL (1/2 tsp.) sugar to first cup and label it "sugar."

3. Add 3 mL (1/2 tsp.) salt to the second cup and label it "salt."

4. Add enough lemon juice to the third cup so it is 1/8 full.

5. Add water to each cup so they are all about 1/4 full.

6. Soak one end of a cotton swab in a random cup so no pattern is established.

7. Gently place the swab on the center, sides, and tip of your partner's tongue to find where the taste is sensed.

8. Record where the taste is sensed.

   Test 1, Cup _____

9. Repeat the test with the remaining cups, using a new cotton swab each time. Remember to record the results.

   Test 2, Cup _____

   Test 3, Cup _____

10. On another piece of paper, make a drawing of the tongue and label the regions as "sweet," "salty," and "sour."

Questions:

1. Where does the tongue have high nerve density? _____

2. What did you learn about the nerve cells in the tongue? _____

3. What other nerve cells have unique functions? _____

_____

Life Science Glossary

genetics—the study of how parents and offspring have similar and different traits

dominant trait—a characteristic that shows physically in offspring

recessive trait—a characteristic that does not show physically in the offspring, although it exists in the genes

heredity—qualities passed on from ancestor to descendants through genetic material

chromosome—part of a cell that contains genes that pass on physical traits from parent to child

vertebrate—an animal with a backbone

invertebrate—an animal without a backbone

bilaterally symmetrical—the left and right sides of the body are alike

organelle—a tiny structure found in the cytoplasm

nucleus—controls the activity of other cell parts

population—all of one species that live in a particular place

sanctuary—a piece of land set aside as a shelter for animals

carnivore—an animal that eats the flesh of other animals

herbivore—an animal that feeds only on plants

omnivore—an animal that relies on plants and animals for food

producer—a living thing that uses sunlight to make sugars

consumer—a living thing that relies on other living things for food

decomposer—a consumer that returns materials from dead organisms to the environment

impulse—a message sent between nerve cells

axon—relays information from one nerve cell to another

dendrites—resemble tiny branches on a tree; receive information from the other nerve cells or from the environment that is demanding a response

synapse—small spaces between the axon of one nerve cell and the dendrites of the next

cerebrum—the largest part of the brain; it controls thinking and decision making

cerebellum—the part of the brain that controls the physical activity of the body

Sample Test

This is a cumulative test containing questions about each of the selections in *Write About Life Science.*

Answer the following questions.

1. What does the study of genetics involve? _____
_____

2. What is heredity? _____
_____

3. What determines gender in humans? What gender does an XY combination indicate?
_____
_____

4. What is the difference between vertebrates and invertebrates? _____
_____

5. Define parasite. Give an example. _____
_____

Match the term with its definition.

_____ **6.** ribosome

_____ **7.** nucleus

_____ **8.** mitochondria

_____ **9.** cytoplasm

_____ **10.** vacuole

_____ **11.** chloroplast

a. jellylike substance that holds all parts of the cell

b. releases energy from the nutrients taken in

c. controls the activity of the rest of the cell

d. where proteins are made

e. food for plant cells is made here

f. contains water and dissolved minerals

Sample Test (cont.)

Answer the following using complete sentences.

12. Do you think plant or animal cells use more energy to live? _____

_____

13. Fill in the Venn diagram below. Compare the two science tools indicated.

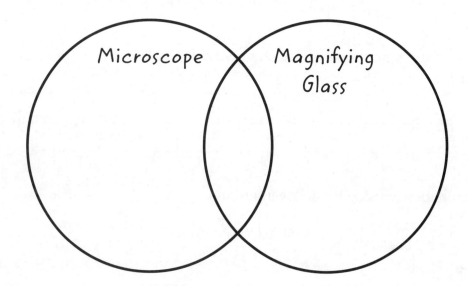

14. Use the information from the Venn diagram to write a compare-and-contrast paragraph about the microscope and magnifying glass.

_____

_____

_____

Fill in the blanks.

15. The _____ fur of the bear indicated it was a brown bear.

16. A _____ eats both animal flesh and vegetation.

17. The grizzly bear is considered a _____ in North America.

Sample Test (cont.)

18. A(n) _____ is any organism that eats something else.

19. When the elimination of a link in a food chain has an effect on the rest of the food chain or food web, we call it the _____.

20. A message sent between nerve cells is called a(n) _____.

Answer the following.

21. Name the three main components of each nerve cell. Explain the job of each component.

_____

_____

_____

22. Label the picture below using the following terms:

- cerebrum
- cerebellum

- brain stem
- spinal cord

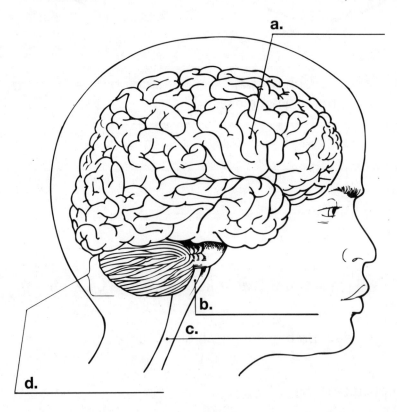

Answer Key

What Do You Remember?.....9

1. The study of how parents and offspring have similar and different traits
2. traits that physically show
3. traits that do not show although they exist in the offspring's genes
4. the passing on of traits from parent to offspring
5. Gregor Mendel. His research showed evidence that traits are passed on through genetic material
6. He used pea plants. They produce a large number of seeds, they are easily cross-pollinated, and they have obvious contrasting characteristics.

Who Is Gregor Mendel? 10

Webs will vary.
Paragraphs will vary.

Who Are You?.....................11

Family trees will vary.
1. Answers will vary.
2. Answers may vary.

Boy or Girl............................12

1. Answers will vary.
2. All egg cells from the female contain a Y chromosome. The sperm cells have half Y chromosomes and half X chromosomes. Therefore, at fertilization, there is a 50 percent chance that a Y chromosome sperm will fertilize the egg.

Inherited Traits 13

1. C
2. U
3. C
4. U
5. Paragraphs will vary.
6. Answers will vary.

Inherited Behaviors..............14

Charts will vary.
1. Paragraphs will vary.

The Meaning of…...............17

1. A vertebrate is an organism with a backbone. A dog, humans, and birds are examples.
2. An invertebrate has no backbone. Examples are sponges, mollusks, and flatworms.
3. fish, amphibians, reptiles, birds, and mammals
4. the left and right sides of the body are the same
5. the spine of an organism; it protects the spinal cord
6. an organism that lives off of another and gives nothing in return
7. Cold-blooded means the blood changes temperature with the air or water surrounding the organism. Warm-blooded means the body temperature stays the same, no matter the outside temperature.
8. a special fold of skin

Concept Mapping Invertebrates 18

Maps will vary.

Animal Adaptations 19

Animals and answers will vary.

Venn Them...........................20

Venn diagrams and paragraphs will vary.

Earthworm's Soil Conditioning 21

1. Answers will vary.
2. Earthworms fertilize and aerate the soil.
3. The composition of the soil might change.

Invert Inventory 22

1. soil type, vegetation, weather, traffic
2. Some may decrease or increase activity. Reproduction may occur.
3. perhaps; some vertebrates may feed on invertebrates.
4. pollution, human occupation, weather conditions

Definitely Cellular.................27

1. where proteins are made
2. jellylike substance within the cell; holds other cell parts
3. chromosomes are found here; controls the activity of the rest of the cell parts
4. holds the nucleus together
5. releases energy from the nutrients
6. controls entry into and out of the cell
7. stores and releases chemicals
8. contains water and dissolved minerals
9. cell membrane
10. chloroplast

Answer Key

What's the Difference? 28
1. Answers will vary but may include the fact that no cell membrane and no chloroplast exists in the human cell. Some parts are the same because the cells must function to support the life.
2. Answers will vary.
3. Answers will vary.
4. Answers will vary.

What Do You See? 29
1. Answers will vary.
2. Answers will vary.
3. Answers will vary.

Very Cheeky 30
1. Answers will vary.
2. Answers will vary.
3. The dye makes things clearer and more defined in the lens.
4. Chloroplast gives plants food. Animals don't make their own food.

Make a Cell 31
Descriptions will vary.

A Special Science Tool 32
a. nosepiece
b. coarse adjustment
c. fine adjustment
d. arm
e. base
f. eyepiece
g. body tube
h. objective
i. stage
j. diaphragm
k. stage clips
l. mirror

Read All About It 35
1. protected area for wildlife and plants
2. the young of a particular animal or plant
3. a group of young born at one time
4. grayish and perhaps fuzzy in appearance
5. a category of organisms with similar attributes
6. a plant or an animal in danger of extinction
7. to take animals by illegal methods
8. eats both animals and plants
9. 700 pounds and 7 1/2 feet tall
10. logging, mining, human development, poaching; answers will vary.
11. You do not want to startle or draw undue attention to yourself.
12. Doing so would keep bears and other wildlife from getting into the food.

A Mammal Too 36
Answers will vary.

Predicting the Future 37
Answers will vary.

Home Sweet Home 38
Answers will vary slightly.
I. Grizzly Habitat
  A. Food Sources
    1. berries
    2. salmon
    3. other vegetation
  B. Surrounding Nature
    1. isolated
    2. woods
    3. water nearby
    4. vegetation
  C. Other Wildlife
    1. salmon
    2. moose
    3. birds
  D. Ideal Climate
    1. cool
    2. dry
II. Endangered Grizzly
  A. How is it happening?
    1. logging
    2. mining
  B. Can it be stopped?
    1. awareness
    2. scientific efforts, including relocation
Answers will vary.

Family Tree 39
Answers will vary.

The Next Few Days 40
Stories will vary.

Answer Key

1. The study of genetics involves research into how parents and offspring have similar and different traits.

2. Heredity is the passing on of traits from parent to offspring.

3. The X and Y chromosomes in the sperm and egg cells determine the gender of the offspring. The XY combination indicates a male.

4. Vertebrates have a backbone. Invertebrates have no backbone.

5. A parasite is an organism that lives off of another organism and gives nothing in return. Examples will vary.

6. d

7. c

8. b

9. a

10. f

11. e

12. Answers will vary.

13. Answers will vary but should reflect the lesson.

14. Paragraphs will vary.

15. grizzled

16. omnivore

17. endangered species

18. consumer

19. domino effect

20. impulse

21. The three main components are the cell body, an axon, and dendrites. Cell bodies contain the nucleus and control the rest of the cell activity. The axon relays information from one cell to another. The dendrites receive information from the other cells or from the environment, and the information is transferred across small spaces between the axon and dendrites.

22. a. cerebrum
    b. brain stem
    c. spinal cord
    d. cerebellum

Answer Key

Look Closer 43
1. organisms that eat
2. all green plants
3. provides energy for everything on earth
4. chemicals used to eliminate pests such as bugs
5. a system, like a chain, by which organisms get their food
6. food chains interwoven together
7. When one organism in a food chain is affected, other organisms in the chain and in the food web are impacted as well.
8. element necessary for life
9. domino effect
10. Answers will vary.

Chain Reactions Everywhere 44
Answers will vary.

Your Daily Menu 45
Answers will vary.

Shop Around 46
1. Answers will vary.
2. Answers will vary.
3. Answers will vary.

Energy Pyramid 47
1. a. Secondary and 3rd-level consumer; eats meat
   b. primary consumer; eats vegetation
   c. living tissue
2. Food chains graphically show food sources. Energy pyramids describe the energy relationships within a food chain or food web.
3. no
4. Answers will vary.

Food for Thought 48
1. five
2. shrubs—insects—insect-eating birds—hawks
3. hawk
4. first-order consumers
5. hawks and mountain lions

Don't Be Nervous 51
1. largest part of the brain; controls thinking and decision making
2. carries out voluntary motion
3. part of the brain that regulates digestion and body temperature
4. controls automatic activity such as blood pressure and heart rate
5. the brain and spinal cord
6. includes the nerves that branch off of the brain and spinal cord
7. messages that travel between nerve cells
8. relays information from one nerve cell to another
9. receives information being transferred from one cell to another and transfers it to the next
10. small space between the axon of one nerve and the dendrites of the next
11. Sensory nerve cells receive the impulses from the nerve cells and transfer them to the brain and spinal cord.
12. Association nerve cells connect the motor nerve cells and the sensory nerve cells.
13. Motor nerve cells send messages to the muscles and glands of the body.

Right or Left 52
1. L
2. L
3. R
4. L
5. L
6. L
7. Answers will vary.
8. Answers will vary.

Find Your Brain Dominance 53
Chart and answers will vary.

Imagine This 54
1. Answers will vary.
2. Answers will vary.
3. Answers will vary.
4. Answers will vary.
5. Paragraphs will vary.

It's a Reflex Action 55
1. Answers will vary.
2. Answers will vary.

Map Your Tongue 56
1. on the taste buds
2. Answers will vary.
3. Answers will vary.